Rambling Man is Moving On

(More Distant Ramblings)

By Andrew D Siddle

Contents

List of Poems

Introduction

A lot of time has passed since I wrote my first poem back in the year 1983. This book Rambling Man is Moving on is my second book of poetry to be published. It brings my poetry up to date by including my most recent work. I've tried to include something for everybody within my writing over the years! My poetry is sometimes New Age Culture , sometimes about classical history, and sometimes about modern day mythology and culture.

Enjoy reading it……..

Rambling Man is Moving on

Rambling Man is Moving on

The title of this poem was inspired by song lyrics once written by J J Cale who I have been a fan of for several decades. He writes and sings rhythm and blues music. Jazz, and blues, and rhythm and blues are music styles that I have had running through my veins, as my very life source, since as long as I can remember.

Rambling Man is Moving on…..A poem inspired by rhythm and blues:-

<u>Rambling Man is Moving on</u>

Moving on down to the Newstead Road,
don't cross the line till you've all been told,
rambling man is movin' on by,
packed my jack and I'll say goodbye.

When wander lust sets you're on your own,
head for the highway to another zone,
think for tomorrow 'cause yesterday's gone,
heading for the sun 'cause you know it's strong.

Don't think of places that you leave behind,
only got the highway to picture in your mind,
tales of travel and the places you have seen,
only takes new boots to start me off so keen.

Never known a time when I've settled in one place,
couldn't care, there's no hurry, it aint a race,
wave bye bye to the people you have seen,
spread your wings, fly high, you know what it means.

For the Love of Heather

For the Love of Heather

Years ago I was inspired by the rock version of the folk song "wild mountain Thyme" by the Byrds and it's mention of the highland wind tossed heather in it's purple shade. Since then I set a little corner of earth aside to grow heather. When it blooms every year I like to sit with a mug of tea and just stare at it. For me it represents freedom of the spirit and is very close to my own raison d'etre.

For the love of Heather

I give my heart to the mountain so free,
the home of blessed Heather there I will be,
purples whites and violets so true,
for joy of the heather I'll be true to you.

Wind over cliff top sings as it could,
the heather it answers as all lovers should,
the whistling and calling unites two as one,
a bonding of spirit till all day is done.

I give my soul for my true kin brother,
the outward sky wind tossed heather & no other,
the sheep that wander through thistle and heather,
for this their haven free without tether.

To the true born wild I come to you,
hill tops peppered and sprinkled with violet hue,
rugged crag and purples always in sight,
to the spirit that lives; nature at it's height.

Passing of a New Age

Passing of a New Age

What is the New Age to you? Is it the 2000 years new age of growth predicted as the Age of Aquarius or is it just a period of general change and technical advancement?

When I was at school some of us were into the song Age of Aquarius back in the early 1970's. For those who remember; it was one of the songs featured on the hit musical film called Hair. I never really lost the desire to be part of that enthusiasm, and thrust, towards advancement in life rather than procrastination. An advancement based on combining high technology, innovation, cultural change, art and music into one all mighty step forward.

Passing of a New Age

The Age of Aquarius for advancement of our fate,
that William Blake predicted in 1809 to state,
a focus on healing and alternative holistic remedies,
east and west together no longer to be enemies.

Our physical world becomes a domain for knowledge & growth,
then the human soul passes to a level away from sloth,
east & west culture infused with part self help,
new holistic remedies designed for better health.

With metaphysics, philosophy, and psychology new to you,
holistic cosmos thoughts for you to see as true,
a "hotch potch" of beliefs said Paul Heelas of this condition,
with an artistic bent and new music to rendition.

New Age Culture may be a higher way to think,
technical and artistic for us without a wink,
a universal change born of single & group development,
that sets most of that before as largely quite irrelevant.

So welcome the New Age and the new thoughts all around,
change for the better and new science to astound,
computer advancement and art that's oh so clear,
a new social order of intelligence not to fear.

A Lidl Bit of Shopping

A Lidl Bit of Shopping

I have been shopping at Lidl Supermarkets since at least 2004. So I thought "that calls for a poem"...and why not a limerick? The Limerick was invented by the Irish mainly for poetry competition writing, pub readings, and fun. Funnily enough invented in a place called Limerick....surprise surprise!

There are strict rules for Limerick writing:-

* It must always be 5 lines long.
* Lines 1, 2 and 5 must rhyme with one another.
* Lines 3 and 4 must rhyme with each other.
* It must have a distinctive rhythm.
* It must normally be funny.

A Lidl Bit of Shopping

When busy shopping out late,
I went into Lidl's for cake,
carrots and peas,
then went down on my knees,
and asked the cashier for a date.

Lindisfarne Holy Island

<u>Lindisfarne Holy Island</u>

Whilst the surname Siddle originally came from the Southern English Saxon terrains it is today thought of as more connected to the histories of north west and north east England. With historic characters such as Siward of Northumbria, in the history books, it would not be possible to be un-interested in the north east with a name like Siddle. This is the main reason that I first developed a fascination with the Holy Island of Lindisfarne. An interest that has proven to be enduring.

Lindisfarne Holy Island

Take my heart to that causeway free,
where the Holy Isle of Lindisfarne be,
shadowed over by a castle mound,
and there on the beach so will I be found.

Give my soul for her celtic art,
knotwork in paint sublime from the start,
and to the wild fowl & seagulls that glide,
high above this Isle where Cuthbert once died.

Saint Aidan your culture brought to the people,
and every week bells toll from the steeple,
for to call all to this special site,
England's secret this celtic delight.

Hilda, Cuthbert, Aidan are three,
Eadfrith & Eadberht all saints by the sea,
Lindisfarne Isle the place where is started,
mice dart through pebbles and grasses are parted.

Sipping mead with a view from the north,
the "Northern Lights" bring magic rays forth,
lighting the lonely waves in the distance,
while Lindisfarne castle shadows resistance.

The causeway cut as high tide rises,
sea water takes the tarmac it prizes,
as the loyal procession of tourists wait,
for the next low tide visitors date.

The Talbot

The Talbot

From the age of 14 onwards, when I first started work a little after my 14th birthday, I was never really seen outside of the company of bikers, biker girlfriends, and hippy/biker type pubs for a few years. I found a happy social enclave within my local pub the Talbot a little later on. The Talbot was a 70% biker and hippy pub adopted by a local motorbike club for meeting up as well. This poem is a happy memory of my local biker pub the Talbot.

The Talbot

Beers on the bar & smiles from landlord Ron',
lined up motorbikes in a line all as one,
Mo' in the corner with ash on his beard,
sawdust on the floorboards and not even weird,

Pint and a whisky downing it down straight,
whacking it down grinning really great,
There's Leslie and his "gal" coming in late,
Claire and her man still bald as a plate.

Playing the jukebox and buying B & H,
Sticking burning matches modeled to be great,
Pool in the making so borrow a cue,
one beer too many and we're all in the queue.

Leslie died when in a motorbike crash,
Claire drifted off time passed with a dash,
Mo's maybe still around but older and grey,
Ron' retired from the lot no longer his day.

So lets now lift a glass and say farewell it's no crime,
to Harborough Bikers and the Talbot pub old times.
now just a new food place and eatery to meet,
but we remember the Talbot and wasn't it a treat?

Ludgate of London

Ludgate of London

In the year 1760 ACE the Ludgate gates to London were demolished. Ludgate had been one of six gated entrances to London city for centuries. The 6 gates to old London were Aldersgate, Aldgate, Bishopsgate, Cripplegate, Moorgate and Ludgate. In later centuries these were also added to by Newgate making 7.

King Lud was one of the first people to rebuild the military walls around London before the birth of Christ. Celtic King Lud is thought to have become a British King around 73 BCE. The original London walls may have been more timber than stone. The Roman Empire went on to credit Lud with being the founder of London City after his death. Hence Lud-Ton/Don became London (old London town). King Lud - The Father of London City.

LUD GATE, THE WEST FRONT.

Ludgate of London

Where did old Ludgate get such a name?
Was it King Lud Lord of such fame?
Six gates to London and Ludgate is one,
named after Lud the King who shone strong.

Son of Heli and the eldest was he,
Androgeus, Tenvantius, his sons for to be,
Lud Deen, Caer Lud, valley or fort?
Defender of London in strategy & thought.

Immortal by masonry of King Henry III,
wondrous stone icons as everyone heard,
Lud in stone with sons both two,
defender of Britain who fought for us few.

So Ludgate sits on Ludgate Hill,
a reminder of Lud a King who will still,
remind us all of a history as found,
rebuilding the walls of London so proud.

Yan Tan Tether

Yan Tan Tether

Up until the 20th century many northern sheep farmers used a strange tally way of counting sheep. The method uses words that are based loosely upon an ancient Celtic Brythonic language but now corrupted. This poem uses the Swaledale sheep counting system. Sheep are counted up to twenty, passed by to the next field, and then another twenty taken and the tally count starts again.

Typically one count would be done every morning and one at the end of the day in the evening for stock control. The language that the counting system is taken from is thought to resemble original Cambric Celtic (in other words from Cumbria in North West England.) although the system of counting was very much part of North Yorkshire Dales life.

Counting up to twenty in the Swaledale sheep herding tally system is :- Yan Tan Tether Mether Pip Azer Sezar Akker Conter Dick Yanadick Tanadick Tetheradick Metheradick Bumfit Yanabum Tanabum Tetherabum Metherabum and Jigget.

Yan Tan Tether

When shepherds of old set out to watch flocks,
they used a tally system to guard their stocks,
a system of tally that came from long ago,
Yan Tan Tether to keep them on the flow.

In old "North Brythonic" they could all see,
count up to twenty then notch it on a tree,
a bit of old bark to tally all that's said,
if you aint got bark then keep it in your head.

Yan Tan Tether is one two and three,
Flossy & Heather and there goes old Dee,
count twenty sheep then round them on by,
then start it all again while the sun is in the sky.

Mether Pip Azer is four five and six,
sheep dog moving and shift 'em through the sticks,
Sezar Akker Donter is seven eight and nine,
Dick Yanadick Tanadick they're moving all the time.

Now thirteen's unlucky for some,
that's Tetheradick on the run,
Metheradick just ran by,
Bumfits lying in a sty.

Yanabum Tanabum Tetherabum's now clear,
that leaves Metherabum and Jigged now to steer,
the whole twenty done and passed to lower field,
then count another twenty Tally Ho to yield.

The Moon Herself

The Moon Herself

Selene and Lah are just two of the many names given to the moon God/dess in classical mythology and culture. Selene is Greek and female....Lah is more Egyptian and male as the spirit Moon God... Also sometimes known as Yah etc.This poem is a dedication to all of those "moon gazers" out there!

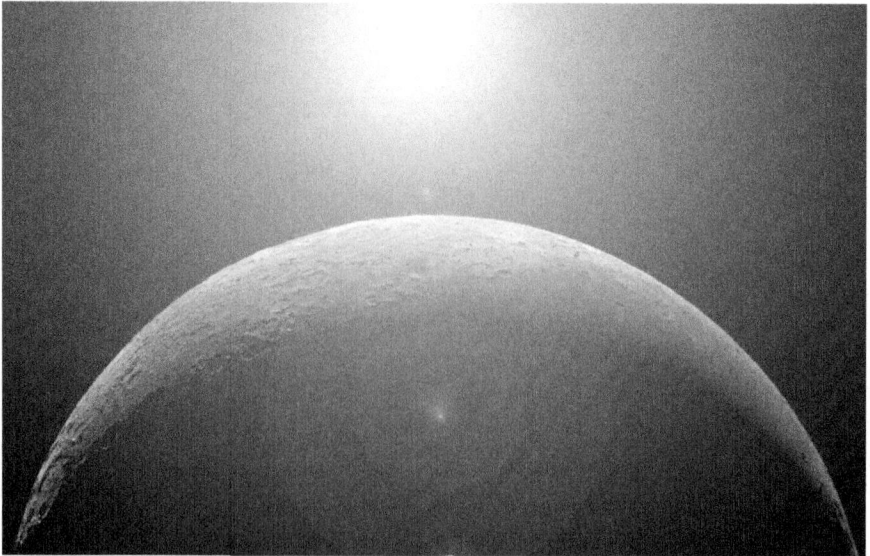

The Moon Herself

Brightest light after the sun,
you were the one when it all began,
staring down on Earth with love,
whilst you spin your dance above.

Are you Selene or are you Lah?
Mysterious shadow of Earth from afar,
full bodied lady or crescent of night,
and once per month your power is at height.

The tide bows down to your sparkling sheen,
Diva of night we know you have seen,
centuries have gone yet we still sing your praise,
and you'll daily rise for the rest of our days.

Pearl of the night your richness is full,
an aura of power that seems never dull,
and hiding in sheets we stare out and see,
to know you fully really can't be.

Gogmagog of Albion

Gogmagog of Albion

Gogmagog is one of the many English Celtic tales of battles and heroism going back to the days when the country was called Albion. Whilst the tale depicts Gogmagog as being a giant; metaphors were always used in early British epic poems and tales. Hence Gogmagog is depicted as being a giant because he was a king and in paintings and drawings would have been shown as being twice the size of his subjects accordingly. This does not mean that he was literally a giant in real life. Giant's leap is also known as Langoemagog.

For those not familiar with ancient British geography Albion was the Indo-European name for Britain. It stopped being used only in the 10th century ACE after Germanic migrants re-named large parts of Danelaw settlement community lands as being Angle-land (England).Originally Albion ran alongside the name Britannia or Britain. Britannia being the Roman Latin name for the country and Al Ban / Al Bion being the name of the country named by the indigenous population. It was called Al-Bion / Al-Ban because the original inhabitants were called Bans and Faiens. Lebanon takes it's name for the same reason. It means "The Ban" or the "Land of the Ban/s".

WILSON'S ALMANAC

THE GIANTS IN GUILDHALL.

Gogmagog of Albion

Albion was a country old,
and for some a tale most told,
old ways said and old lores,
so little new upon her shores.

The people there were ruled by fear,
by a few giants who would steer,
threatening and ursurping they rampaged the land,
the people being small never made a stand.

Then one day a fleet of ships landed,
a group of battle torn soldiers banded,
fleeing from Troy and the war now gone,
headed for Albion's sands to belong.

Now this band of Troy were ruled by Brutus,
Corineus got Cornwall to stop it being useless,
there to rule and plant crops new,
living in peace in hope for his few.

So headed by Corineus a feast was staged,
with Ale and culled sheep that they'd caged,
seeing the smoke of the cooking of meat,
a problem then arose to spoil such a treat.

Gogmagog was a giant of Cornwall,
one of the last leaders so scornful,
the strength of his arm was mighty great,
he could rip out a tree one armed if irate.

Now Gogmagog led his giants to the feast,
to smash those of Troy & force them to cease,
and Corineus cried as tables now smashed,
his people being battered right to the last

Gogmagog was tough and 12 cubits tall,
and so very few could ever make him fall,
Corineus didn't cease despite 3 ribs smashed,
fearing that Brutus his King would be lashed.

With ribs broken Corineus's rage grew,
'till out of the door he raged and now flew,
flinging Gogmagog up into the air,
he carried him off with a most manic stare.

Lifting higher and running with speed,
up to the cliff by the shore like a steed,
at the cliff top with a force not known,
over the rocks Gogmagog was thrown.

Brutus was delighted by Corineus's deed,
& gave him fair Cornwall for to plant seed,
from that day on until the last peep,
Gogmagog lies under Giant's Leap.

Universal Harmony

Universal Harmony

The concept of yin and yang became popular with the work of the Chinese school of Yin yang which studied philosophy and cosmology in the 3rd century BCE. Yin and Yang philosophy of cosmic harmony has been in use since at least 700 BCE. Basically Yin is a feminine form of energy and Yang a masculine form of energy. The two forms of energy pervade every aspect of life , being, and object be they inanimate or animate. There are no physical dividing lines between Yin and Yang and the two can cross into each other or even change from one form of energy to the other. But the truth is that there is a constant controlled adjustment to ensure that there is just the right amount of each energy form to create balance or wholeness. This may be macro balance in the cosmic universe or micro balance within the inner self.

In Chinese mythology "yin and yang" were born from chaos when the universe was first created and they are believed to exist in harmony at the centre of the Earth. During the creation, their achievement of balance in the cosmic egg allowed for the birth of Pangu (or P'an ku), the first human.

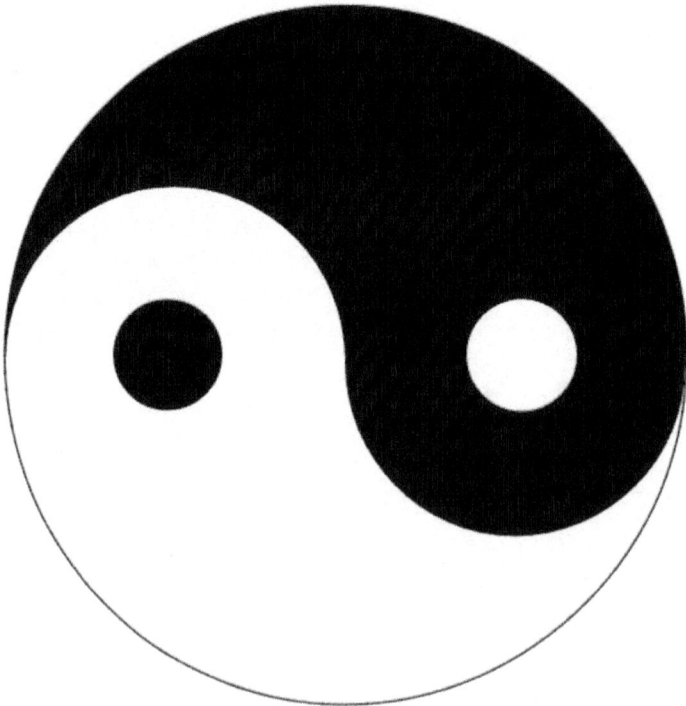

Universal Harmony

Seven hundred years before the start of Common Era,
came a universal harmony thought to be much clearer,
balancing & re-balancing the seasons change as one,
a universal architecture or Yin and Yang begun.

Night and day are opposites hence part of Yin & Yang,
Totality of wholeness in a Universe seen by man,
the seed of Yin enters the form of Yang also,
crossing over boundaries so to create the whole.

No dividing lines only opposites thrusting through,
nothing is absolute and nor or me and you,
an interpenetrating relationship of balance to the end,
opposites become equal but cross and can extend.

Yin and Yang the automatic balance of all being,
to understand the wholeness of a theory that's all seeing,
so harmonise body & mind with equal flow of thought,
emotions and spirit then balanced as I exhort.

The King Has Gone

The King Has Gone

This poem is a tribute to B.B.King who died on thursday 14th May 2015 at 9.40 p.m. in the evening......May he rest in peace.

I have been a fan of blues, and rhythm and blues, for quite some decades. From Cream to the Yardbirds, to early Fleetwood Mac, to B.B.King & J J Cale. I love it all.

The King Has Gone

Where have you gone to our King of blues and style,
9.40 on Thursday you left and flew the mile,
over to the other side where Angels stomp the beat,
and Cherubs re-united play base lines in the heat.

250 shows per year you played most of life,
and only when at 80 did you reduce that 'cause of strife,
your Gibson Guitar called Lucille reached the highest note,
when playing "The Thrill Has Gone" you really got the vote.

The Chicago stage saw you fall ....they thought their King had gone,
But you strolled on another year to show that you were strong,
then one evening bright the angels took your soul,
to play a "distant gig" up in the Heavens whole.

With 15 known children you kept your family strong,
and all the while still singing the guitar notes never wrong,
so millions of "Blues Fiends" now applaud your 50 plus albums left,
though millions who also saw you....... are left now most bereft.

Tammy Tang Ton

Tammy Tang Ton

Tammy Tang Ton......Why did I write this? I really don't know!

I Probably wrote it because both during my time at East London University in the 1980's (previously East London Polytechnic) and The University of Birmingham we had a couple of Chinese girls in our study group. So I kind of got used to having Chinese girls around me all of the while...what better reason to write a poem about a Chinese girl.

Tammy Tang Ton

Tammy Tang Ton was a Chinese girl,
the cutest sway that I ever did know,
walking on behind with a glint in my eye,
hips that rock make a man feel high.

Hair so black and long to her waist,
lips so full it's a real disgrace,
as the sun goes high it's a full blown treat,
watching our Tammy slink down the street.

When in a store to buy for the week,
the guys stutter and go kinda meek,
puppy paws bent when she hands them the change,
then a sway of the hips it's really kinda strange.

tightest jeans that you ever did see,
glossed up mouth the fullest there could be,
worlds collide for a good looking gal,
that's Tammy Tang Ton just a walkin' down the mall.

Tammy Tang Ton was a Chinese girl,
the cutest sway that I ever did know,
walking on behind with a glint in my eye,
hips that rock make a man feel high.

Hay Day

Hay Day

When I was at school I sometimes forgot to load my P. T. kit in my bag on mornings when we were due to have Physical Training. Anyway what used to happen during the rugby season, sometimes, is that a group of us , without P.T. kits, would sit by the side of the pitch to keep out of the way.

I found myself surrounded by rather a lot of farmer's sons, who had also forgotten to bring their kits, to school …….and the conversation always turned to rural things, wild life, and tractors. I guess that is what inspired this poem.

Hay Day

Basil Grummidge knew a thing or two 'bout corn,
his dad always said "he'd know'd it since wa' born",
and every now and then when on a tractor in the field,
people would stop and say "by gum...his future's sealed",

So young Basil struts through the mud tracks on the way,
followed by a Muntjac and field mice from the hay,
heading for the top field fresh manure to spread,
and here comes young Daisy bouncy and well fed.

Daisy knew Basil when he was only eight,
and racing sticks down stream they'd always get home late,
but now full bodied Daisy knows a different kind of race,
and sometimes around midday they vanish without a trace.

So here comes the midday sun bringing Skylarks on the rise,
the wildness of nature below the azure skies,
and there go Daisy & Basil always hand in hand,
the geese start gaggling; laughing at all that's planned.

Northampton Castle

Northampton Castle

By the time of the battle of Northampton Town,UK,
in 1264 odd things were going on. At various stages
Parliament meetings were being held at Northampton Castle for
the Nation. A Royal Mint had been established within
Northampton Castle walls to produce coinage for the nation. Also
a consortium of renegade intelligentsia from Cambridge
University, Oxford University, Canterbury and others had set
themselves up in the centre of Northampton town to teach new
ideas and philosophies not approved by the crown.

After the battle of Northampton the town shops, university, and
other buildings were almost burnt to the ground by King Henry
III. The castle was also attacked and walls smashed in the
siege by siege machines. Northampton Town was later banned
from having a University of it's own for several centuries. This
was for fear of another uprising brought about by radical thought
and ideas being taught to the town's people.

View of the NORTH GATE OF THE CASTLE (from Sepia drawing in Abington Abbey Museum,
date and artist unknown). On the southern side of Fitzroy Street is an old stone wall, with a gateway.
Just within this wall was the old Moat of the Castle, and on entering the gateway was, at one time, to
be seen the view here reproduced, making some allowance for artistic conceptions. The position of
this North Gate is well shown on the map.

Northampton Castle

Once there stood such a long time ago,
the pride of Northampton that so few know,
solid walls of sunblest stone,
Northampton Castle as built for the throne.

Built of timber then later of stone,
a magnificent castle on a mound of it's own,
The Earl of Northampton Simon De Senlis,
in Northampton his men did defend this,

A building so strong that it housed the mint,
coins for the nation's production stint,
the Northampton revolt of 1264,
King Henry raged and hit them sore.

With siege machines pulled from the south,
5th of April they stood open mouthed,
Simon De Montfort was thrown from his horse,
Henry the third was victor of course.

Torching shops and the University proud,
Northampton was almost burnt to the ground,
Simon's army was captured as well,
and many were burnt in the growing mell.

For centuries on from that day forth,
Universities were banned from this town "up north",
and Parliament never again did hold,
their Chamber debates in this town so old.

As walls crumbled and fell to decay,
the memory of power just faded away,
with the final memory of castle walls gone,
Northampton's people then just carried on.

Lighthouse of the Mind

Lighthouse of the Mind

Back in the early 1980's I decided to buy a black and white trendy Les Paul "repro" electric guitar. Also a load of special effects equipment and rhythm box, and an 8 track recording deck to start to write songs. I didn't get very far because I later decided to become a property Consultant instead. Never the less at the time I wrote a song called the Lighthouse. This is more or less what the the words were to the song and I think it reads better as a poem than sung as a song in hindsight. In the original song version the first four lines were the chorus which was repeated over and over again throughout the song. The words were originally inspired by the James Taylor song the lighthouse but I wanted to produce something with more of an Alan Parsons Project style music backing and drum beat. Anyway here is the poem - Lighthouse of the Mind.

Lighthouse of the Mind

Far from the distant shore,
I see a lighthouse burning gold,
and as a moth is to a flame,
I see my life pass by once more.
The tide smashed walls they stay,
memories and scars of old,
and as a lighthouse shines through night,
I resolve to continue to fight.
For every ravaged blasted stone,
that lighthouse grew in hallowed strength,
with only one purpose true,
to see the night ships pass on by.
So now I see my only truth,
to let my ships pass by unharmed,
to hold on solid to my truth,
and never let light dreams die.

The Epic of Nann Shlea

The Epic of Nann Shlea

Imagine a new series of stone cuneiform tablets found in the area that was ancient Mesopotamia. What excitement would there be in translating the words into modern English? Now imagine the disappointment if the translation of the ancient epic turns out to be just a little bit of silliness!

New translation, from Cuneiform stone tablets to English of the Epic of Nann Shlea. Sumer , 1st period, Cuneiform.

The Epic of Nann Shlea

Hey Nay Knoo,
it's the way that we do,
and they tickle Tammy Toe by the door.

It's the way that we say,
just a Tommy Tie day,
'cause it's all been said just like before.

Say Sammy Slea,
'cause it's the right way to be,
but there's really no Troatta to the core.

Tammy Tang Tied,
it's a really long ride,
then you're right up to the top for some more.

If they don't say it's Kireau,
then it's a whole load of Direau,
for the Slingo slopes Freago for the score.

Hey Nay Knoo,
it's the way that we do,
and they tickle Tammy Toe by the door.

Spirit of the Oak

Spirit of the Oak

This is a Cinquain poem (pronounced Sin-Cain). This is a type of poem first invented by Adelaide Crapsey around 100 years ago in the USA. The Cinquain has set rules as to how it should be written:-

* Cinquain poems must be 5 lines long.

* A Cinquain poem has 2 syllables on the first line, 4 on the second, 6 on the third, 8 on   the   4th, and 2 syllables on the 5th line.

* Cinquain poems do not need to rhyme but can if one wants to.

Spirit of the Oak

Tall Oak
is hard and tall
high above one and all
feeling so small under his might
in fright.

The Curse of Tam Lin

The Curse of Tam Lin

Tam Lin is a famous folklore story of Scotland based around Carterhaugh. Carterhaugh is an actual place with woodland and river in Scotland. This is my version of the famous epic poem based upon the original tale.

Wikipedia:-

Tam (or **Tamas**) **Lin** (also called **Tamlane, Tamlin, Tomlin Tam Lien, Tam-a-Line, Tam Lyn,** or **Tam Lane**) is a character legendary ballad originating from the Scottish borders. It is also associated with a reel of the same name, also known as Glasgow Reel. The story revolves around the rescue of Tam Lin by his true love from the Queen of Fairies. While this ballad is specific to Scotland, the motif of capturing a person by holding him through all forms of transformation is found throughout Europe in folktales. The story has been adapted into various stories, songs and films.

The Curse of Tam Lin

A long time ago lay a Hall so grand,
called Carterhaugh in the woods didst it stand,
the family Mackenzie held it dear,
and loyal to it's walls without a fear.

But some years gone a young man whence,
vanished in the woods in total suspense,
and the family Mackenzie in fear did flee,
for Tam Lin had gone; no longer was he.

For the fairy Queen did steal his soul,
and tag it to the woodland grove,
for 7 years his spirit shall stay,
and guard the woodland from rising fray.

On the 7th year Halloween,
Tam Lin's soul shall be paid by the Queen,
as fine from her to the Gates of Hell,
Tam Lin's soul then will leave the Dell.

Tam Lin - Guard of the wood

_____

One clear and bright young morn for good,
young Janet was given Carterhaugh wood,
but her father told her succinctly and clear,
stay away from the whole place in genuine fear.

Tam Lin's spirit guards the Dell,
and will not see you stand by it's well,
maids have come and maids have gone,
Tam Lin will let them pass by none,
without a fee of one personal thing,
or take a maidenhood with a fling.

Now Janet was stubborn and stout hearted she,
would no longer listen or obey he,
into the woods she went without sound,
and stood by a well that she had found.

Reaching down to a rose there grown,
she plucked it away from it's thorn born home,
flashing lights and flames then abounded,
and the fairy guard bugle perfectly sounded,
in a flash of light that came from Hell,
Tam Lin appeared at the woodland dell.

Janet felt no fear at all,
arguing she owned this Carterhaugh,
so Tam Lin true to his spirit form,
stole her maidenhood and left her torn.

Fleeing away from this woodland scene,
Janet thought of what she had seen,
but finding now a baby due,
she resolved to return and see it through.

Returning back to Carterhaugh wood,
to search for herbs to stop as she could,
her baby to be born out of the wood,
as she searched for herbs just as she should.

Tam Lin again and not just "slightly",
seeing Janet and declared most rightly,

"You will not kill; that would be frightly!"

" Our baby shall be born of this wood,
  nothing shall stop it; understood?"

Then Tam Lin told her further more,
to save him from entry to hell's own door,
on Halloween she must see him right,

and drag him down from his horse in spite,
of the Queen of Fay to whom he shared,
his very soul of which Janet cared.
Declaring love they swore that day,
that Janet would win and Tam Lin would stay.

Descent to the Mortals

So the night of Halloween and a procession drew,
to the woods of Carterhaugh and the fairy few,
Janet now hid right out of sight,
waiting to do her deed this night.

First came a black horse then came a brown,
then a white one and Tam Lin to be downed,
flinging her green mantle around his frame,
he was flung off his horse with no thought of blame.
and holding him down she hoped and she prayed,
to bring him back mortal for the love that she craved.

In her arms his image changed into a bull,
then burning with fire and the flames filled her full,
The loudest of screams came from demons of Hell,
until finally human he eventually fell.

Seeing the curse at last had been smashed,
the Queen of fay fell and her fairy horse slashed,
and looking back upon Tam Lin to see,
she saw Janet and he run for to be.

Screaming in bracken the fairy queen said,
if I'd have known; you'd never have been fed,
I'd rather pluck his eyes than let you run free,
and plant them with growth from the oldest oak tree.

Had I have known you'd steal our fair Tam,
I'd have plucked out his heart and so be damned,
for in it's place I'd have given a stone,
with no heart at all for you to own.

With this Janet and Tam quickly ran,
never to share with the Queen of the damned,
and now again mortal Tam Lin was free,
so never to the woods would he ever be.

Give me Stripes / M & S Shuffle

Give me Stripes / M & S Shuffle

This is a poem inspired by Marks & Spencers stripy shirts. I haven't got a lot to say about it really because it speaks for itself........So to "stripy shirts" ....and why not!

<u>Give me Stripes / M & S Shuffle</u>

I've tried white and cream and also blue,
but they're not stripy so really won't do,
a shirt that'll "hurt" with stand alone "heights",
without my striped shirt I'd have sleepless nights.

To be a "cat" whilst out on the razz,
you have to have stripes to give them the dazz,
and at work what's the point in plain white starched,
when stripes on the collar get all of their backs arched.

Preening my "whiskers" with stripes blue and red,
for a night at the club instead of off to bed,
and as the jazz saxophone increases it's pitch,
I'll polish my cuff links just like the Lynx.

So "purring" for green stripes from M & S,
I'll visit the mirror to pass for the best,
of all the good things given to man,
there's "nowt" like a striped shirt......the rest be damned!

Swallowed by a Book Worm

Swallowed by a Book Worm

From the earliest I can remember I can remember references to "a right little book worm" from school regarding people who read too many books. Being somebody who has a vivid imagination I just thought "but what if book worms are actually real creatures"! Hence was born this poem.

Swallowed by a Book Worm

I was reading my book called Gilgamesh,
peace and quiet whilst reading to cherish,
when out of the next page,
flew in a rage,
a book worm with barely a blemish.

Well I sat with my mouth open aghast,
for my fate was already cast,
it swallowed me whole,
right down its great 'ole,
and I sank to its belly so fast.

I sat amongst its last night's meal,
thinking now what's the big deal?
I'd not be out of luck,
had I not read that book,
so perish Gilgamesh I feel.

The moral of this tale you see,
will leave you pale as can be,
when reading a book,
it's best first to look,
for signs you're a bookworm's next tea.

<u>Street Life From a Front Window</u>

Street Life From a Front Window

Watching the world go by outside has always been a pre occupation with me. For many years I have worked from or studied property & land law academia from home. The thing about working from home is that it is essential, in my opinion, to have a window either overlooking the garden or overlooking the street scene outside. It is just about being in tune with what is going on around oneself really. It is like a form of meditation in itself ; just tuning in to what is going on around whilst still doing one's work.

Street Life From a Front Window

Watching all the world as it bungles on by,
couldn't care less if you really know why,
seeing all the folk just wandering down the hill,
here comes a courier ; his name is (unpaid) Bill.

A kiddies ball rolling by a milk bottle crate,
fancy a game of footie; it really would be great!
Stoking up the energy to weed the front drive,
and stay away from no. 6 it really is a dive.

Milk floats, old blokes, prams and baby cries,
haven't filled the bird bath; it's really rather dry,
chintzy cats stroll beyond places they should be,
picking up a street chat & listening in for free.

Refuse collectors smash lids in common time,
join the rhythm calling it's really rather fine,
removals of furniture move away with no. 3,
deliveries from Sainsburys ; and now it's time for tea.

Watching all the world as it bungles on by,
couldn't care less if you really know why,
seeing all the folk just wandering down the hill,
here comes a courier ; his name is (unpaid) Bill.

Madrigal

Madrigal

I wrote this with intention for it to be a modern Madrigal

A Madrigal is a lyric poem suitable for being set to music, usually short and often of amatory character, especially fashionable in the 16th century and later, in Italy, France, England, etc. (a short lyric poem of medieval times). The Madrigal was orignally popular in Italy and later moved over to Britain.

madrigal ('mædrɪgəl) / Farlex Free Dictionary

1. (Classical Music) music a type of 16th- or 17th-century part song for unaccompanied voices with an amatory or pastoral text.

2. (Classical Music) a 14th-century Italian song, related to a pastoral stanzaic verse form
[C16: from Italian, from Medieval Latin mātricāle primitive, apparently from Latin mātrīcālis of the womb, from matrīx womb]

Madrigal

When the swords, now struck, leave you bled and dry.
Dry your tears, wipe your eyes, for each thwarted step you've seen.
Come away to the land, in the swirling mists, and leave your folk to fry.
Come away to the living, forget the dead,where for love of you I have been.

When the dragons of Mount Never Now,turn their back, and are blown away.
When the seeds of life, blowing with the wind, gather the sweetest of musk.
Ask yourself why, with any thought of you, I held you close to stay?
I come to you now, with lance held high, and with me you'll be before dusk.

I'll lay you down , to the mystical bower, your dark hair unfurling like reeds.
Of all that hurt, of times so curt, we will fly above so keen.
Open your wings, and open your heart, I heed now to your pleads.
Of years to come , you'll stay as young, for time past seemed so mean.

So I'll polish my breast plate, and oil stone my sword, cutting down all with venom.
Your life to cherish , so let them perish, turn to me and run.
Now we see, with our Madrigal key, not with robes, but wearing denims.
For your freedom now, you must see it's how, that's our Madrigal finally sung.

When the swords, now struck, leave you bled and dry.
Dry your tears, wipe your eyes, for each thwarted step you've seen.
Come away to the land, in the swirling mists, and leave your folk to fry.
Come away to the living, forget the dead, where for love of you I have been.

Mount Never Now

<u>Mount Never Now</u>

When I was a toddler I was fed on a literary diet of fairy tales about distant lands and mountainside retreats. Mount Never Now is surely one of those places that exists as a beautiful idyll somewhere at the back of the mind. Somewhere at the back of the mind far away from every day chores and the mundaneness of everyday life.

Mount Never Now

A mist soaked morning on Mount Never Now. Early morning frying bacon smoke fills the air breeding quickly broadening hunger pangs. In the distance flows a bustle of people with morning chores and mountain burdens to bear.

A day in the life of Never Now Mountain. Early dawn bell tolls gather the faithful to prayer. In the midst of this far away happening what know they of us so far far away.

Birds circle above with mocking calls. Waiting for the chance to pick off seedlings from the carefully crafted mountainside terraced fields. In the midst of the village a spurting fountain. Gushing of water trickling almost all day.

Pantiled roofs of the reddest river bank clay stand over yellow stone picture post card homes. Seemingly precariously balanced on the mountain side but safe on their own plateau. The road winds down from Never Now Mountain and slithers , serpent fashion, into the distant lowlands. Almost hissing in it's serpent appearance before vanishing into the distant horizon below the low lying sun.

Hanging Gardens of Babylon

Hanging Gardens of Babylon

A poem about the Hanging Gardens of Babylon. One of the legendary 7 wonders of the world...The Hanging gardens of Babylon. Created for Princess Amytis, who missed her home country, by her husband Nebuchadnezzar II.

Hanging Gardens of Babylon

Of all the wonders of the state,
and the joy of Amytis as fate,
to Babylon a garden new,
with hanging flowers and fervent views.

Poor Amytis she missed her home,
though her husband ne'r left her alone,
so a new garden planned for her to see,
all the flowers and shrubs of her home country.

Palm trees and the rarest flowers,
selected and trimmed for many hours,
and waterfalls from the greatest heights,
whilst baskets swung from left to right.

Cultivation from within the air,
whilst passers by just stopped to stare,
the brightest range of coloured plants,
with violets, reds, and golds that dance.

So the evening sun breeds a Babylon breeze,
backed by the rustle of leaves in the trees,
and shadows now grow their heading home hearts,
as gardeners stroll by with high laden carts.

Sunday Snoozles

Sunday Snoozles

What are Sunday mornings for? Sunday mornings are for dozing in bed with a cat on your head whilst waiting for the paper boy with the Sunday morning news. Sunday mornings are for somebody else to bring you your morning cuppa tea because it is Sunday. Sunday mornings are for bacon and toast smells.....and going back to bed because it is too early to get up.

Sunday Snoozles

Sunday bells and "Sunday Times",
newspapers abound to background chimes,
the wind sings sweetly to the morning sun,
sitting in bed with the newsprint done.

Dozing "Dees" and pillows snug,
mid morning tea and dog on rug,
bacon, beans, fried bread and egg,
don't get up eat the lot in bed.

Lawn mowers in the distance roar,
morning prayer on Radio Four,
somewhere in the distance stands,
a queue for church to hear God's plans.

So when do we make Sunday dinner?
Another snooze then I'll be on a winner,
snoring lightly 'till the click of a door,
alright I'll get up don't be such a bore!

What's the Time Grandad?

What's the Time Grandad?

Before I entered the years of puberty , as a teenager, I used to go to visit my grandparents in Darlington City from time to time. In fact this often used to amount to a two week holiday. Their names' were Reg' and Edith Siddle. Reginald was rather special because back in the 1920's and 1930's he was a soccer star for both Spennymoor United and the Darlington City Quakers team in North Yorkshire / County Durham.

Reg' had two regular mannerisms with myself. One was to wack me really hard around the head with a rolled up newspaper if I tried to sit in his fireside rocking chair. The other was to say "half past bacon" if I ever asked him what the time was because he objected to "clock watchers"!

Right up until a few years before his death Reg' was always followed around by both teenage girls , and some older females as well, when ever he went out because of a local memory of his earlier football star sports days. This became quite embarrassing because local girls used to walk up to him when he was even in his seventies standing at a bus stop.

What's the Time Grandad?

What's the time grandad?
it's half past bacon,
can I sit in the rocking chair?
it's already taken.

Lifting up a rolled up newspaper,
for a wack around my ear,
I was sitting with a silly grin,
and it wasn't even fear.

What's the time grandad?
It's half past bacon!
Can I sit in the rocking chair?
It's already taken.

Tales of Spennymoor soccer scores,
and Quakers training done,
all of my time wondering,
what it was like to be that one?

What's the time grandad?
It's half past bacon!
Can I sit in the rocking chair?
It's already taken.

All of those years of age,
yet they still stop by to say,
you may be in your seventies,
but your with us all the way.

What's the time grandad?
It's half past bacon!
Can I sit in the rocking chair?
It's already taken.

Acrostic

<u>Acrostic</u>

This poem is called "Acrostic". Strangely enough because it is an acrostic! An acrostic is a
poem or series of lines in which certain letters, usually the first in each line, form a name, motto, or message when read in sequence.

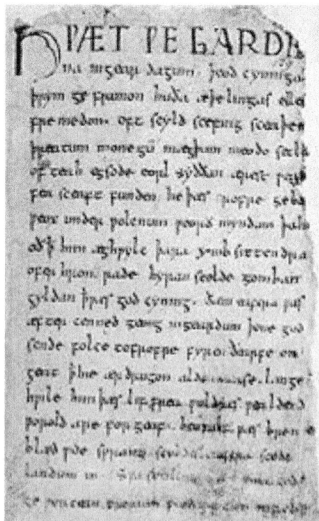

Acrostic

T   he heart of a soulful poem
H   ides some true epicentre of
I   ndividual human expression.
S   ophisticated or simple doesn't really matter.

I   t is the raw essence of emotion, even
S   pirituality, that makes a poem work &

L   ife experience cannot be replaced by
I   nsular technical knowledge of poetic styles
F   or a poem to be a genuine, soul felt,
E   xpression of feelings and memories.

The World's End

The World's End

This Poem is about the World's End pub at Ecton in Northamptonshire. The World's End Pub had a known historical use back in the English Civil War when it was converted into a prison and Mortuary to house Royalist prisoners and their dead. In the years since 1645 poltergeists and spirit sightings have been more common at this pub than anywhere else within Northants County (arguably).

The World's End

The World's End Pub at Ecton pub of glory,
some who have been don't believe the story,
a long while ago came the war in 1645,
the Battle of Naseby and those who lost their lives.

The World's End Pub marked the end of the line,
Royalists were held there & told to bide their time,
their treatment was bad and even more fell,
more and more dying when the landlord rang the bell.

The beer cellar converted and staffed as a mortuary,
but had you seen the dying you'd see it was a slaughtery,
calling time each day the landlord made a notch,
another dead tally and a royalist in the stocks.

Many years on and the pub crowd sit and wait,
footsteps from the cellar & the dead walk round the crate,
a half bodied walker marches through the floor,
and a skinless faced nun appears just as before.

A happy party crowd back in 2002,
sat with their beers and nothing much to do,
then flashed and flickered an image of the nun,
some ran and some stayed as nothing could be done.

The World's End Pub at Ecton Northants,
A Spirit with your beer sir? So watch the dead dance,
of Cavaliers and Round Heads you'd think they'd all be
gone, but at the World's End Pub you'd be completely
wrong.

<u>Kelpie of the Loch</u>

Kelpie of the Loch

Prior to the conversion to Christianity in the British Isles the Kelpie was a very common part of folklore all over Scotland. A horse like water spirit that acted as a localised God like guardian of the rivers, and lochs, and lakes. A spirit that could shape shift and change into human form from time to time as it wished.

<u>Kelpie of the Loch</u>

The white crested waves smashed to the shore,
mirroring turbulent times in store,
then white turned to "mane" and "neddying" strong,
out walked the Kelpie in the midst of this throng.

Tossing her head back with a shake of her mane,
water tossed off to the shore with a strain,
and crunching of hooves on pebbles so loud,
but this spirit of water stood proud on the ground.

Then making a noise like Niagara Falls,
her image changed as an onlooker called,
shifting of shape from a horse to a girl,
but beware the hair of river reed curls.

The most beautiful fountain of youth was she,
curves to die for and legs for to see,
but beware the hooves that still show she,
as the water horse guardian & spirit so free.

Triumph of Horus

Triumph of Horus

This poem is about the tale of Horus, the son of Isis and Osiris, in old Egyptian folklore and religion.

In the poem Geb and Nut where the parents to four children. The children were Osiris, Isis, Set, and Nephys. This was at a time when it was acceptable for a queen or king, of old Egypt, to appoint their own brothers and sisters as joint throne holder (hence wife or husband).Geb was the sky God and Nut was the Earth Goddess.

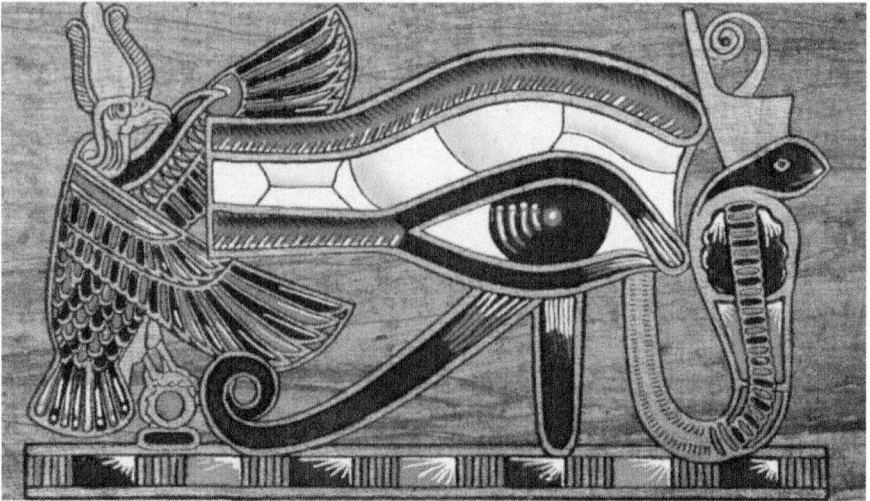

Triumph of Horus

Children of Geb & Nut

Isis was begot of Geb & Nut,
wife of Osiris whose future was cut,
sister of Nephys and Set from the start,
Isis the lady of the broken heart.
For as her husband Osiris was King,
Set her brother stole everything,
transforming himself to a monstrous form,
Set smote Osiris and killed him by dawn.
Spreading his innards and body fair,
around old Egypt without a care,
with Osiris dead Set was now King,
master and controller of everything.
As new master he made Nephys his queen,
sister and Pharaoh his equal as seen,
Isis she cried for Osiris for days,
his body parts scattered through valleys & maize.
So Nephys felt sorry for Isis in tears,
and decided to help her cure all her fears,
to search for the limbs of Osiris the Dead,
then resurrect the man and blow life to his head.
Finding her love once more to be mortal,
Isis fell pregnant and Osiris now chortled,
a son was begot and his name was Horus,
the people all cheered they are surely for us.

The contest

Now Horus was jealous of Set the King,
his stolen crown didn't mean a thing,
so Horus decided to take the throne,
a Royal Egypt to rule alone.
A contest was arranged for the right to govern,
on a steaming hot day that felt like an oven,
but Set he cheated in all contest events,
so Isis she trapped him in early moments.
Set pleaded in earnest for to spare his life,
and Isis then freed him for all of her strife,
her son Horus now burst into rage,
is this true life or are you all on a stage?

Horus and Set then agreed one more trial,
for the right to kingship they would race for a mile,
in a boat race for two for all to see,
who should be king and ruler so free.

Horus declared to make things hard,
each boat should be stone or else be barred,
Set built a boat from mountain rock with glee,
but Horus new it might never be,
building his boat of timber and smothered,
with finest of limestone; plaster was covered.

The boat of Set it sank like a rock,
the Gods they laughed at this stupid clot,
so raging with fury Set rose with spite,
transforming to a "hippo' Horus to fight.
Smashing his boat; but Horus was tough,
fighting off Set in a battle so rough,
but the Gods had enough and stopped the fight,
So who should be King and what would be right?

Court of the Gods

A court was formed of Gods all above,
to lobby Osiris from all of their love,
and who should be King will you tell us please?
Osiris of the underworld; who should hold keys?

So Osiris the Dead stated quite true,
no Kingdom by murder! So Set is now through,
Egypt's throne was never caught,
by an act of murder and perish the thought.
So now I bequeath Kingship to Horus my son,
the Gods agreed and that's Horus won.

So Horus took the throne and all in all,
Egypt's power fell to his call,
and it was said all over the land,
Osiris now rests for his son is grand.

To Work or Not to Work?

To Work or Not to Work?

I have often thought about the meaning of the word work and what it actually means to people in contemporary society. Is it a source of inspiration or just a chore? Should everybody have career ambitions or should it just be for the purpose of earning enough dronga to pay one's living week to week bills.

Here is the poem.....To Work or Not to Work.

To Work or Not to Work?

If I reach for the stars what would I find,
Would life be better than the stairs on the way,
Climbing up slowly with a true state of mind,
but once at the top what would I see the next day.

Is it better to have worked or to labour on still,
Joy in vocation or retirement day,
If nothing is there once up on the hill,
then is life better with simple joys to stay.

Is there reward in winning or fulfilment in labour,
So is the choice of mankind to say,
a communal voice of opinion to savour,
is it better to leave or stay in the fray.

So as you develop your craft to working perfection,
feel the strains of life give way to bliss,
feel the joy of creating without correction,
your role on earth confirmed by God's kiss.

Jack in the Green

Jack in the Green

The Jack in the Green was a major part of pre-christian beliefs in Britain. After the advent of Christianity old Jack merely became embodied within Carnival like, once yearly, celebrations that remembered him alongside Christian rituals. Jack represents the coming of spring and is the very spirit of spring's being. Jack is the one who carefully breathes life into newly sown seeds and newly grown saplings till they flourish with full green force as spring moves on to summer every year.

Jack in the Green

Opening the curtains slowly one morn,
spring's new young spirit to be seen after dawn,
when between two daffodils sprang forth the chap,
Jack in the Green doffing his cap.

Springing in two step with half visible face,
seeds for the new grown sprayed around with grace,
darting through Bellis he vanished without trace,
then reappeared with a big smile daisies in place.

My hands they trembled with this apparition of spring,
his vision in morning starts the flowers to sing,
and oh to believe that flowers scream their delight,
singing and a swaying whilst I hide out of sight.

This happy time party of plants , spirits, and weather,
brings forth the sunrise and the newly flowered heather,
old Jack completes his daily tasks before dusk,
then ascends back to Otherworld beyond garden's cusp.

Haggling Tom Grey

Haggling Tom Grey

This is a light hearted bit of fun. It's a poem about a wheeler dealer called Tom Grey and his philosophy for a good life......Nuff said!

Haggling Tom Grey

Hagglin' Tom Grey,
had a theory so they say,
and it carried him through to the end.

If you haggle every price,
you'll be doin' rather nice,
and they'll never say it's all pretend.

Every deal done,
should be battled to the core,
then always offer two never four.

When it comes to your life,
never take a full sized wife,
a smaller one will cost you half the food.

If you want a new car,
never travel too far,
not a Rolls when a Reliant Robin's good.

When old Tom died ,
his family firmly said,
not a coffin when cardboard box we'll send.

Hagglin' Tom Grey,
had a theory so they say,
and it carried him through to the end.

Charon's River Crossing

Charon's River Crossing

This is a poem about the mythical ferryman Charon.

Wikipedia

 In Greek mythology, Charon or Kharon (/ˈkɛərɒn/ or /ˈkɛərən/; Greek Χάρων) is the ferryman of Hades who carries souls of the newly deceased across the rivers Styx and Acheron that divided the world of the living from the world of the dead. A coin to pay Charon for passage, usually an obolus or danake, was sometimes placed in or on the mouth of a dead person. Some authors say that those who could not pay the fee, or those whose bodies were left unburied, had to wander the shores for one hundred years. In the catabasis mytheme, heroes – such as Heracles, Orpheus, Aeneas, Theseus, Sisyphus, Dionysus, Odysseus and Psyche – journey to the underworld and return, still alive, conveyed by the boat of Charon.

Charon's River Crossing

Someday The Gates of Hades wait,
for me to wander through as fate,
and Charon to his master's call,
will carry me through the water's trawl.
What truly makes life's turbulent flow?
Eddying of time till time to go,
flowing from year one until the last,
and still I see my turbulent past.
If I could hold back time I would,
turn Charon's ferry back if I could,
to see Hades's furious raging face,
with no ferry boat to the Pearly Gate.
Years come and years go,
a "trumbling" treadmill but still I know,
if I could cancel this flow on by,
I'd do it now with head held high.
So now in the distance a mysterious light,
the tunnel to Charon's river in sight,
but not now my friend I'll bide my time,
Hades will have me not I'm fine.

H.M.R.C. Fun Time

H.M.R.C. Fun Time

As somebody who is self employed I have always had to do my own annual accounts and tax calculations for H.M.R.C. It is a task that all self employed people have to do and all self employed people must surely hate. Anyway; here is a poem about that lovely, lovely, organisation called the H.M.R.C. and their requirement for an annual return.

H.M.R.C. Fun Time

Tax time again and the figures done,
Gross and Net and not for fun,
National Insurance Class Four & Two,
churn it all out and wait in the queue.

Now online tax that's the stuff,
16 digit i.d's just to be tough,
I've remembered my number so time for a rest!
Phew, that'a tiring, i'm lacking in zest.

What happened to those tax guys who used to wear bowlers?
If you don't get your skates on they'll fit you with rollers!
Tax deadlines are dates to be abhorred,
if you don't fill the form in they knock on your doors.

Oh Beautiful tax claim my net profit is hot,
net assets to view and that's not the lot,
oh praise be the inspector who says "where's the rest?"
but that's all you'll get so I haven't messed!

Tax time again and the figures done,
gross and net and not for fun,
National Insurance class four & Two,
churn it all out and wait in the queue.

<u>Tuned in to Water</u>

Tuned in to Water

When I was a teenager I started looking into various things to do with spirituality and meditation. In fact I actually received tuition in the art of meditating with a view to entering what is known as the Astral Plane. I was taught that the easiest way to relax and start to slow one's breathing & body systems is to imagine a stream flowing or tide breaking on the shore. The image in the mind is relaxing and helps create a feeling of inner peace to then further build upon. That is why this poem is called tuned into water.

Tuned in to Water

When you sit by a river feel the calm of her flow,
see the scene in all from your Pineal glow,
when hearing the froth of her turbulent force,
cover your ears hear the sound from within of course.

To feel nature's spirit without vision or sound,
pure inner eye and pictures inbound,
deep within your inner most mind,
see all that is there & all you can find.

Reduce your breathing with every new breath,
count each one till heavy breathing has left,
peaceful and tranquil as the river flows by,
feel the power of knowing with the deepest of sigh.

Now see the New Age grow from deepest of sight,
and spirituality give you new found might,
meditation focuses all that you be,
new found strength in a person so free.

Do You Remember Cuddlekin Jones?

Do You Remember Cuddlekin Jones?

Since the age of 12 I have been engaged twice, married once at Kettering Registry Office in Northamptonshire, had two daughter's by different women and one son, plus intend producing, or adopting, more in the future.

Of my existing children only one survived who now has a family of her own and lives in the Kettering district of Northamptonshire. This poem is a memory of all of my years of girlfriends, fiances, engagements, breaking off engagements, and the female form since I first started dating females at the age of 12.

Do You Remember Cuddlekin Jones?

Maxine was my first we walked home every week,
in shapely skin tight jeans she made me feel so meek,
Sue held my chest her fingers felt so good,
but we were way too young we knew we never could.

Tina was so keen we agreed to marry our fate,
but when I went away we knew it was too late,
Jo' was the best for social days out,
but when it was off we'd scream and shout.

Later came Sharon her blonde her to the ground,
buried in her curves I never could be found,
and what happened to Zoe my cuddlekin pet,
soft and curvy and the best I've met.

Oh ...and long ago Julie who came from a farm,
If her father had known he'd have done me some harm,
for all the girls that I've ever held near,
to the feminine form that I hold so dear.

Our Creed

Our Creed

I am an Orthodox Catholic Christian so this is a poem taking elements of the Orthodox Creed in a different way. Basically I just decided to take the Creed and fragment it; then use various lines pasted back together in the form of a poem. Here is the poem......Our Creed.

Our Creed

To believe in one is to truly belong,
begotten before ages or you'll be wrong,
after the Father and light of light,
if you don't believe you'll be lost in the night.

One Lord Jesus Holy Spirit or Ghost,
giver of life to you we shall toast,
the Holy Catholic & Apostolic Church,
united as one we no longer search.

For remission of sins we became baptised,
and in His Holy Name we reach for the skies,
begotten son you were never made,
and in his name we all were saved.

So now we look to the world to come,
worry ye not or you'll be quite numb,
the dead's resurrection is plainly spoken,
so in your life enjoy this Creed token.

The Eye

<u>The Eye</u>

So…..what is this poem about?

A long time ago one of my first loves in life had to have both of her eyes removed, having had various health complications, and having been poisoned with a brain parasite normally found in under cooked fish. She changed from somebody with blue eyes to somebody with brown eyes over night as the brown ones' were the only ones available for her. At the same time I also have a fascination with the third eye, or Pineal Gland, due to the fact that I was brought up in the midst of 1960's culture, alternative beliefs, and an understanding of the third eye in connection with meditation and the Astral plane. This poem is about eyes. It jumps from thoughts of my love's blue eyes and on to thoughts of the third eye and meditation.

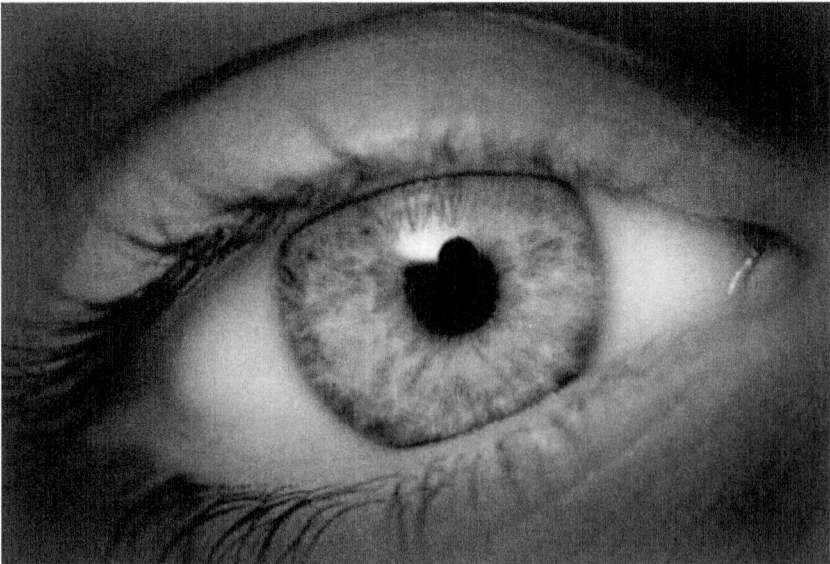

The Eye

The eye I once saw that smiled from your soul,
a mystical vision of thoughts never told,
why did you leave all that innocence behind,
you were never to know all that you sought was so blind.

An eye of inner being high up above,
an inner sense of seeing transcends above doves,
the knowing of the living and a sense of human kind,
a feeling of wisdom in all that we find.

Your eyes of blue were a reflection of truth,
those beautiful deep pools of deepening proof,
why did you leave me those eyes to now go,
you were not what they saw and this you well know.

The sound of wind howling lifts up all of our minds,
seeing enlightenment brings many new finds,
viewing it all from a far away glance,
feeling and showing as returning from trance.

Sweet Talking Mollie

Sweet Talking Mollie

I have always enjoyed talking to women on the
telephone. In some ways the play between a man and
a woman in words is the raison d'etre for life within a
true male. After all what was a man placed on the
earth for......We were placed on earth to create a
chemical reaction that creates a life spark in a blink of
an eyelid. So lets celebrate the difference between
male and female and celebrate the girlie phone call
even more so......

Sweet Talking Mollie

She came on the phone quite late in the day,
I'd been busy working so hadn't much to say,
then my hand started to tremble as she lowered her voice,
sweet talking Mollie just left me no choice.

Sweet young Mollie knew a thing or two,
when chatting up men she'd never wait in the queue,
how can a word sound so like a caress,
imagining she's sitting there undoing her dress.

The voice of a Muse from long ago times,
those sensual words as if she now pines,
to make me feel special by sentence or pitch,
without even planning it's really her kitsch.

So there goes Mollie.... Princess of the phone,
the way that she phones makes her never alone,
my meals now burning because of her call,
but hey.....when she's talking I'll let it all fall.

<u>Return of the May Queen</u>

Return of the May Queen

The May queen is another of those quintessential features of original British culture prior the advent of Christianity.

Wikipedia:-

In the **High Middle Ages** in England the May Queen was also known as the "Summer Queen". **George C. Homans** points out: "The time from **Hocktide**, after **Easter Week**, to **Lammas** (August 1) was summer (*estas*)."

In 1557, a London diarist called **Henry Machyn** wrote:

"The xxx day of May was a goly May-gam in Fanch-chyrchestrett with drumes and gunes and pykes, and ix wordes dyd ryd; and thay had speches evere man, and the morris dansse and the sauden, and an elevant with the castyll, and the sauden and yonge morens with targattes and darttes, and the lord and the lade of the Maye".

Return of the May Queen

Spring time and the Dandelions gleam,
smiling yellow faces or so they seem,
daisies burst from down below,
singing "we're here" & we're going to grow.

Sow your seed to the morning sun,
time for growth and new born fun,
the spirit of spring gently blows,
the breath of life on all that she flows.

Apple trees burst with new shown green,
the "Queen of May" is now to be seen,
slowly blowing life to all around,
as she regally passes all to astound.

Sun rise and sun fall,
nature's cycle to one and all,
the flame of life to a tune on high,
as all seek answers from the sky.

More George

More George

"More George well what could that possibly be on about Andrew?...Oh you really have gone too far! ......Well it's about more George see innit?"

I've always fancied doing my own rendition of George and the Dragon and it would be most inequitable to not do so whilst living in the region called England of the Uk.

So here it is! ...Yep... erm... oh yes......Here it is.... "More George" :-

More George

Cappadocia lay in the fairest place,
that gave birth to our George in grace,
young George who once was in Siline,
the sun beat down and the streets so clean.
The people drank from the local pond,
in this city of which they were so fond,
but then one day that pond was spoilt,
and the people's right to drink was foiled,
for there coiled round a dragon roared,
poisoning water as if so bored.

In fright they sacrificed their own,
first sheep, then men, then young ones known,
till one day for the latest slaughter,
they requested for the King's own daughter.
Crying sadly "no not mine",
but the people screamed we have no time,
if not your own we'll scream and shout,
then burn your house and force you out.
So the King's own daughter was tied and bound,
and led to the dragon without a sound,
crying by the pond in tears,
nothing could relieve her fears.

Now came George with lance and sword,
a Red Cross Knight he crossed the ford,
and to the pond in high dismay,
to hear the maid cry on this day.
"Go your way lest you perish in Hell",
but George he knew and knew fair well,
raising his sword he slashed his blade,
to the dragon's scales a cut was made,
crimson blood ran right down,
the dragon's sore and not a sound.

George asked the maid to tie a belt,
and lead the dragon on as felt,
to the city hall for all to see,
how George had set the people free.
The King was proud his daughter grand,
the dragon stopped and so be damned,
but George refused money and much more,
saying "I have no need" and "what for?" But
to finish the dragon do me one thing,
baptise to Jesus let the people sing,
then set up a church in the name of he,
and let the people sing of the free.
Then raising his lance high in fury,
he rammed the dragon through quite
purely,
and the people bowed and started to pray,
the church of Jesus was set that day.

Nigel's Nose Flute

Nigel's Nose Flute

I remember at the age of about 7 having a discussion with my classmates about what it would be like to play the nose flute. I don't know why but the conversation just seemed to flow that way! All of these years on I can honestly say that I never did get to have a go at playing one......so I've written a poem about playing one instead.

Nigel's Nose Flute

From o'er the fields and beyond yonder moor,
cometh a magical sound like n'er before,
wherest did'st it come from I hear all of ye ask?
Oh , it's our old Ruth's young 'un, completing 'is tasks.

Flaring his nostrils till they almost burst,
filling his lungs till they really hurt,
then blowing a tune like a soft angels tongue,
that's Nigel and his nose flute, he's played it since young.

Changing 'is nostrils from both left to right,
playing it higher with all of 'is might,
cross eyed and high pitch with a nasal blown core,
his hair fringe now flying with each nose blown score.

So o'er the fields run bulls , sheep, and man,
traversing so fast now, as quick as they can,
to see the true source of music so sweet,
that's Nigel and his nose flute; it'll never be beat.

Sandwich on the Dashboard

Sandwich on the Dashboard

The kind of work that I have always preferred involves travel. I personally have lived, or worked, in many different counties and anywhere from Lancashire to East London…..Indeed anywhere between Derby and Ely, Birmingham City, Leicester City, Nottingham City, Northampton, West Ham and half a dozen others or so I guess! Who is counting anyway? I can tell tales about different people and different places. My need to travel, within my blood, came first and the suitable job for a travelling type came later.

Sandwich on the dashboard

Sitting in a layby on Watling Street A5,
lorries front and back and it's good to be alive,
straighten up my tie in the mirror nice and neat,
then drive off in my "Chevy" faster in the heat.

Why doesn't everyone love the open road?
Freedom of the carriageway instead of doing what you're told,
first call is a rent appraisal 3 floor multi let,
then a court visit the bookings all been set.

My leather pilot case stuffed with green files,
driving by gated fields with people climbing stiles,
foot down on the accelerator change to 5th gear,
cloudless sunny day ahead and the road is almost clear.

Sandwiches and lucazade that's lunch for field staff,
on the way to a re-possession I'm late so it's no laugh,
Finishing off the working day at 8 then on a date,
68 hours per week but I like it it's my fate.

Blue Morning

Blue Morning

Blue Morning! What could be better to start the morning of a confirmed rhythm and blues fan than blues music I ask you? So to all blues fiends out there this is another new morning and another blues music poem.

Blue Morning

I woke this morning and felt a sadness deep inside of me,
so turned on some music and let the saxophone set me free,
guitar solos that grind and reach a height,
but without my baby I'll still be alone by night.

Looked out of the window & the sunshine turned to rain,
without my honey there's no Heaven only pain,
the day you left I tried with all my might,
but the blues they took me firmly out of sight.

So I listen as the drum beat starts to roll,
playing slowly the music hits my soul,
sitting on my own I saw no future to be,
then the blues came to call and set me free.

Blues vibrates inside my very bones,
feeling all things in turn to be alone,
'till some new found "gal" calling on to me,
the blues they finally got to let me be.

Planning a Kitchen Herb Garden

Planning a Kitchen Herb Garden

I have had an interest in the medicinal properties of herbs, and their use in food, since at least 17 years of age. I have always viewed it as being part and parcel of the culture that I am part of. Starting with the 1960's hippy era and developing/moving on to modern New Age Culture with an interest in animals, flora and fauna, and the nature of our planet at large.Anyway where ever I live people normally find at least a few herb plants......so this poem is all about my love of herbs and need to have them where ever I live.

Planning a Kitchen Herb Garden

Planning a herb garden is a pretty hard chore,
which species to buy to be at the core,
I know there's Parsley, Rosemary, and Sage,
and maybe a little something to help in old age.

The smell of Lavender is always nice,
and I like Coriander so I'll be planting it twice,
Common Thyme was recommended but it's as I said,
who are you calling common....you're out of your head!

Feverfew could be handy as a brew of tea,
Lungwort I don't know I don't think it's for me,
Cowslip boiled up hot; freedom from sleepless nights,
maybe not Henbane; Hyoscine just kills with fright.

Lemon Balm would be good I'll stink the house with tea,
Juniper I don't know so I'll have to wait and see,
Fennel is fluffy and really good to hold,
then Rue for my view if I'm really bold.

Planning a herb garden is a pretty hard chore,
which species to buy to be at the core,
I know there's Parsley, Rosemary, and sage,
and maybe a little something to help in old age.

Beyond the Depths of Danu

Beyond the Depths of Danu

When Christianity first came to ancient Albion there was a brief turning point in culture before the old faded and the new ways arose. The turning point marked the loss of the British Indo European race in the name of the newly labelled anglo-saxon race. Prior to Christianity there were many Vedic Aryans in the British Isles. The form of Brahmanism that these white Asians followed included a memory of the Goddess Danu; a primordial Goddess who still appears in the Rigveda of India.

When Britain converted to Christianity there was a need, within some, to protect their older tales , Goddesses, Gods, and culture. This was carried out within the tales of King Arthur. Here the Vedic Aryan Goddess of the Waters becomes the Lady of the Lake who took back the sword Excalibur from Arthur and disappeared back into the water. So the Vedic Aryan beliefs were actually preserved , and not lost, within the Arthurian legends, et al, for the future. Excalibur symbolises the sword forger "old Thor" of Mesopotamia. Thor was the man who historically first invented the battle sword for war and in so doing became a King through superior ability. A lot of the ancient culture and beliefs of old Albion were preserved in tales for the future. One just has to know how to interpret the stories, and folkore, to realise this.

Beyond the Depths of Danu

A still lake with muddy depths,
deepest brown with ripples in steps,
now and then a hint of blue,
reflected sky prisms mirror the view.

A Swan glides by with cygnets three,
Mallards quack their paddles free,
Algae heaves both up and down,
Frogs meander their sploshings found.

Did I imagine or did I see?
Way down below the watery quay,
a glint of treasure from long ago,
gold well hidden for us to know.

What lurks beneath those murky depths,
was it sun's reflection or treasures kept?
By the Lake's Lady of long ago,
Danu of the waters concealed stow.

Trees surround in solemn stance,
gentle waters beyond the land,
a rowing boat stands right in sight,
as the midday sun "sloths" to it's height.

Wheat Sidhe

Wheat Sidhe (Pronounced Shee)

Many tales both in Britain and Ireland revolve around good people or the fairy folk. In Ireland the word Sidhe (pronounced Shee) literally means the good folk, or fairy people, in Gaelic. In India the word also exists but becomes Siddhe in parts of Asia. In Mediterranean countries the word often "shape shifts" to the phonetic equivalent Sidi. However the word Sidi means Saint or community leader in the religious sense. Hence one can either take the word Sidhe to mean a good person or a saint. I would have said that both definitions are one and the same, if thought about carefully, when discussing ancient folklore and the meaning of words! Here is the poem…..Wheat Sidhe:-

The Wheat Sidhe

The sky clouds swirled unusually grey,
the sun fragmented in splinters arrayed,
then the eeriest of whistles in the wind set forth,
so the Sidhe of the wheat came with a force.

This half visible creature, translucent, she smiled,
long blonde hair that she flicked all around,
mischief to make as she blew with all might,
a circular hole in the wheat out of spite.

Then gathering strength in her flowing white dress,
she span around and caused much distress,
a flame ball from her heart to the core,
and rose to the sky with a roar but what for?

Trying to hide I bowed right down low,
but the wheat sheaves parted she stood on tip toe,
peering out at me with half visible smile,
I turned to run and head for the mile.

In the distance behind I heard her laugh,
and the wheat it blew in the growing winds gaff,
so headed I for the tavern far away,
far from the pretty Sidhe shown that day.

Today has Gone

Today has Gone

This is the final poem of this book so it is time to end the book and end the day. Sit down, with feet up, and dwell upon the events of the day and wonder what tomorrow is likely to bring. Thanks for reading.

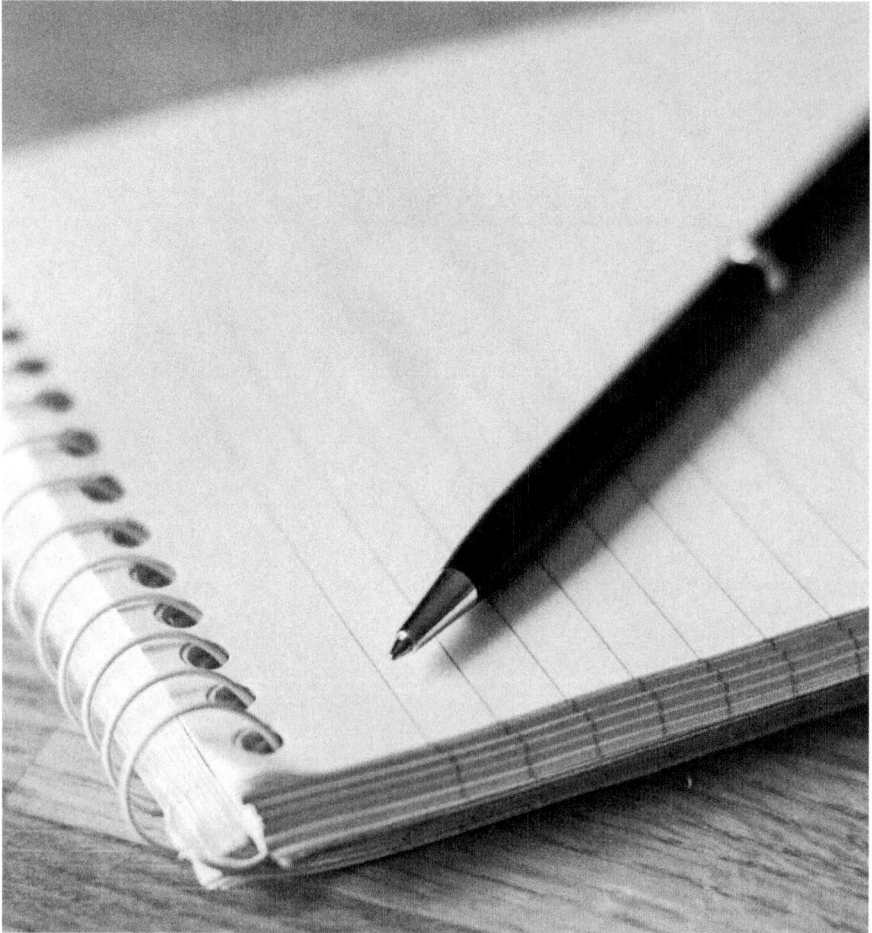

<u>Today Has Gone</u>

Tomorrow will be a good day I think,
today has gone & the hours left shrink,
with the few hours left I bide my time,
Radio Four and a glass of wine.

What did I really achieve today?
My work, and a poem, nothing else to say,
one man amongst so many,
what footprint in time left if any?

But to strive to leave a trace of thought,
is a marvelous thing if one contrives the right sort,
a footprint of memory or feeling by pen,
maybe one day to be found by fellow men.

So let us just see how the words flow with time,
the reasoning simple with no thoughts sublime,
another small poem to finish the day,
then float off to dreamland until the new day.

Acknowledgement

Thank you to all the people who have given me the life experiences needed in order to be able to create this book. Thank you to all the people within all the locations that I have lived in since the year 1966:-

To the communities of Lancashire and especially Padiham. To the communities of Birmingham City and especially Harborne. To the communities of Leicestershire and especially Market Harborough. To the communities of East London and especially West Ham. To the communities of Northamptonshire and especially Kingsthorpe. Thank you.........

Printed in Great Britain
by Amazon

85273470R00122